D0241840

Forest Life

and Woodland Creatures

DK

DK | Penguin Random House

Senior designer Hannah Moore
Editor Violet Peto
Fact checker Wendy Horobin
Photographer Mi Elfverson
Senior producer Isabell Schart
Producer, Pre-Production Dragana Puvacic
Jacket designer Amy Keast
Jacket coordinator Francesca Young
Managing editor Penny Smith
Managing art editor Gemma Glover
Art director Jane Bull
Publisher Mary Ling

First published in Great Britain in 2017 by
Dorling Kindersley Limited
80 Strand, London WC2R 0RL

Copyright © 2017 Dorling Kindersley Limited
A Penguin Random House Company
10 9 8 7 6 5 4 3 2 1
001–296395–Mar/17

All rights reserved.
No part of this publication may be reproduced, stored
in or introduced into a retrieval system, or transmitted, in
any form, or by any means (electronic, mechanical,
photocopying, recording, or otherwise), without the prior
written permission of the copyright owner.

A CIP catalogue record for this book is available
from the British Library.

ISBN: 978-0-2412-7311-1

Printed in China.

A WORLD OF IDEAS
SEE ALL THERE IS TO KNOW

www.dk.com

Parents

This book is packed with activities for your little ones to enjoy. All projects are designed to have an adult present. Please be safe and sensible – especially when you're doing anything that might be dangerous (or messy!) Have fun.

Contents

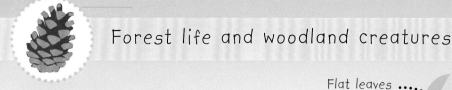

What is a forest?

Flat leaves

A forest is a big wooded area where lots of trees grow close together.

Tree types

There are two main types of tree in the forest. There are **deciduous** trees that have flat leaves, and **coniferous** trees that have thin and spiky needles.

Deciduous trees lose their leaves in autumn. They mostly grow in places that don't get very hot or very cold.

4

Forest creatures

Forests provide food and a home for many creatures. Animals eat the nuts and berries that grow there, and use the trees to make their nests.

Coniferous trees are usually green all year round. They can grow in hot dry places, and in cold snowy mountains.

Thin spiky needles

Cone

Cones come from coniferous trees.

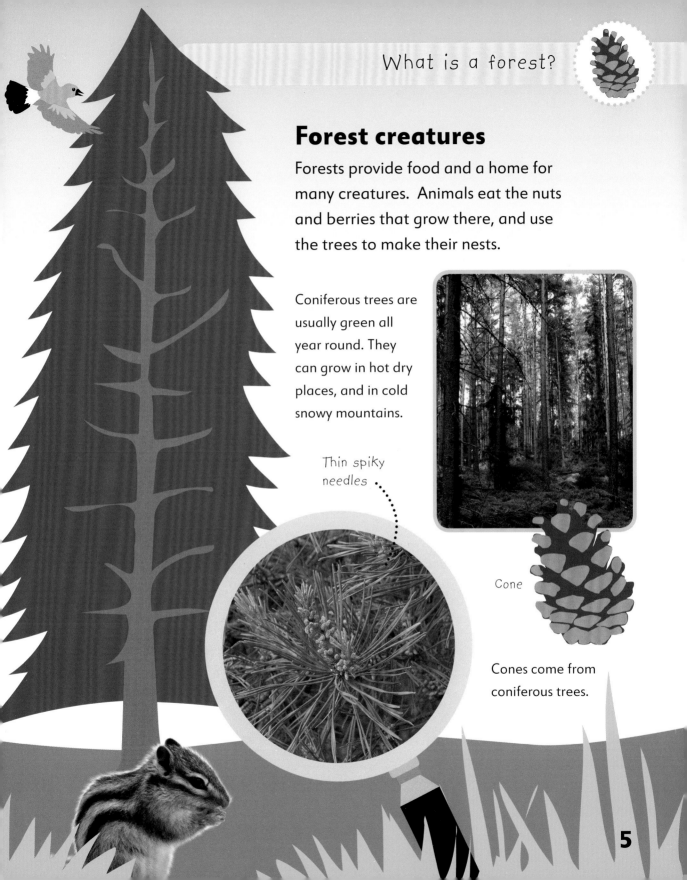

5

Leafy bugs

Collect **leaves**, seeds, and **grasses** from outside and create a leafy buzzy bug.

You will need:

A collection of leaves, seed cases, grasses, and flowers of different sizes

Modelling clay

Toothpick

1

Arrange your collection into matching pairs. Set aside a piece of modelling clay about the size of a golf ball.

2

Roll the clay into a sausage shape for the body. Poke a leaf into each side of the body to make a pair of wings.

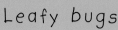

Bug friends

Use the rest of your nature collection to make friends for your bug.

3

Poke the rest of the leaves into the clay. Use different-coloured smaller leaves on top for extra decoration.

4

Add your antennae. Prick the clay with the toothpick to give the body a bumpy texture.

7

From seed to tree

Even a **huge** tree starts its life as a tiny **seed**. Just like you, trees grow taller as they get older. **Oak** trees take more than a hundred years to become fully grown!

1

An **acorn** grows...

Every tree has seeds. Acorns are the seeds of an oak tree.

2

When an acorn falls to the ground, it grows roots and a leafy green shoot.

..... shoot

..... acorn

..... roots

...into a **seedling**...

8

Did you know?

Trees have a hard skin called bark. It protects them from weather and hungry animals.

3

...then into a **sapling**...

4

...and finally an adult **tree**.

Raccoons have long sharp claws that help them climb trees.

The high life

Many forest animals live **high up** in the trees where they make a **safe** and cosy place to raise their babies.

Dreys

Squirrels scurry up and down trees carrying twigs. They use the twigs to build a nest called a drey.

Dens

Raccoons often use an empty hole in a tree as their nest, which is called a den.

Chicks that have grown feathers are called fledglings. This means that they are ready to learn to fly.

Woodpeckers peck into trees to find juicy insects or to make a nesting hole.

Birds' nests

Many birds build their nest in tree branches. They make them with twigs and grass which the birds weave together. Sometimes they use mud or spit for glue.

11

Plate nests

Go outside and find **materials** to make your own bird's nest. Look out for **feathers**, twigs, grasses, and **leaves.**

You will need:
Paper plate
Blue paint
Paintbrush
Nest materials
PVA glue
Coloured card
Scissors
Cupcake case
Googly eyes

Paint the top half of the paper plate sky blue and wait for it to dry.

Get your nest materials ready. Then cover the bottom half of the plate with glue.

Now stick on your nest material as shown here.

4

Ask an adult to help you cut a *beak*, *tail*, and *legs* from the coloured card. Fold the cupcake case in half.

5

Add *blobs* of glue between the two halves of the cupcake case and stick in the pieces of card. Stick on a googly eye.

Magpie nest

Cheeky magpies are known for stealing sparkly objects for their nests.

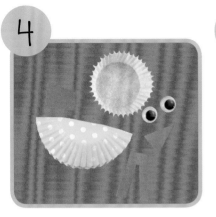

Try adding shiny buttons and beads to make a magpie nest.

Glue your bird onto the plate. Add eggs and a sun to finish your picture.

13

Forest feast

The **plants and trees** in the forest provide a whole feast of different things for animals to eat.

Berries

Animals are attracted to the bright colours of berries.

Buzzing bees suck the sweet nectar from flowers.

Crossbills have a beak that is specially shaped to hook out seeds from inside cones.

14

Nuts

Animals that eat nuts need strong beaks or teeth to crack hard shells.

Seeds

Seeds grow inside a protective casing. Animals pick out the seeds to eat.

Flowers

Insects munch on leaves and petals, or eat the nectar made by flowers.

Did you know?

Some of the berries, nuts, and seeds that we find in the shops come from the forest.

Lots of animals, such as deer, like to eat juicy berries.

Chipmunks are nutty about nuts!

15

Berry ice lollies

These delicious **ice lollies** make a refreshing treat on a hot day.

You will need:

150g (5½oz) mixed berries

2 tbsp runny honey

300g (10oz) plain yogurt

Ice lolly moulds

You can use any mix of your favourite berries.

Blackberries

Raspberries

Blueberries

1

Put the mixed berries into a bowl and mash them with a fork.

2

Pour the honey into the bowl of berries and mix together.

Place a spoonful of berry mixture into each ice lolly mould followed by three spoonfuls of yoghurt. Repeat until full.

Once the ice lolly moulds are full, put on the lids. Put the moulds in the freezer for at least four hours before eating.

Caution

Not all wild berries are safe to eat. Always check with an adult before picking or eating them.

The clean-up crew

Slithery bugs and slugs **clean up** by eating dead leaves and wood from the forest floor. Without them, forests would be piled **high** with dead plant life!

Fungi make a special juice that breaks down dead leaves and wood.

The layer of dead leaves is called leaf litter.

How many woodlice can you count?

Woodlice

If you look under a piece of dead wood, you will probably find woodlice. They like to live in damp and dark places.

1

2

3

4

Earthworm

Worms eat dead plant life. They turn it into vitamin-filled poo which plants soak up to help them grow.

Stag beetle

Stag beetles lay their eggs in dead wood. Their babies eat the wood when they hatch.

Snail

Snails cut up leaves with their special tongue called a radula. It is covered with thousands of tiny teeth!

7

8

9

10

5

6

Worms make tunnels deep in the soil, which helps water to reach plant roots.

Bug hunt

When you are out and about, look under dead leaves or wood. Which bugs can you spot?

19

Bunny burrow

Rabbits dig **tunnels** called burrows using their strong legs. A **warren** is a group of connected burrows.

Rabbit warren

Warrens often have lots of entrances and exits. There are special areas for babies, and for sleeping.

Baby area

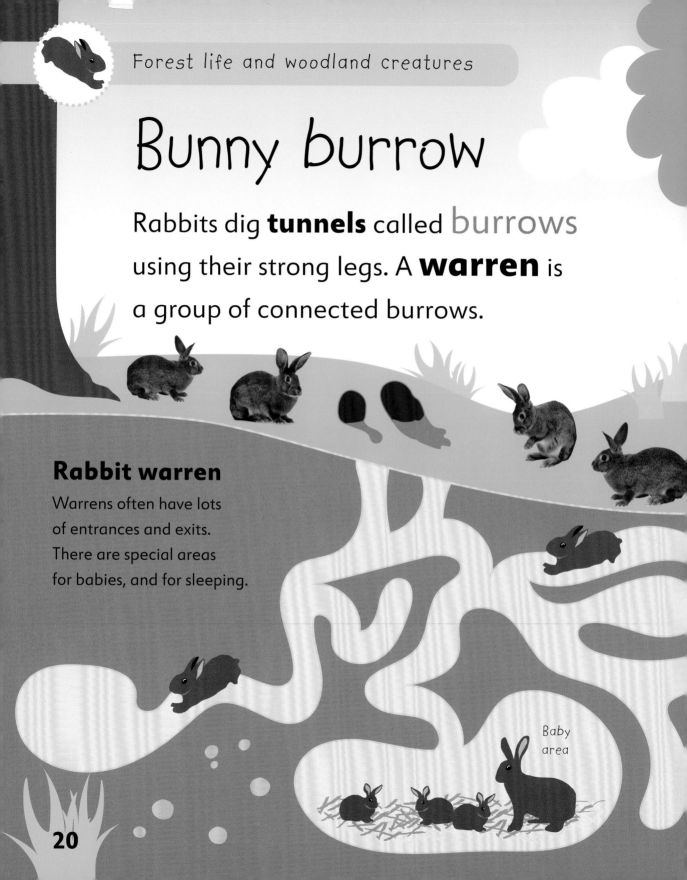

Bunny burrow

Did you Know?

A female rabbit can have as many as TWENTY babies in one year!

Start

Can you help this tired bunny find her way to the sleeping area?

Happy families

Rabbits live together in large groups. There can be many families all living in the same warren.

ZZzzzzzzzzzzzz

Sleeping area

Finish

Into the night

Each night when you go to sleep, many woodland animals **wake up**. They have super **senses** to help them hunt and get around in the **dark.**

Who is hiding in a hole in this tree?

Foxes

A fox can **hear** mice from a long way away, then it creeps up and pounces!

Wolves

An excellent sense of **smell** means wolves can sniff out their dinner.

Porcupines

Sensitive hairs on their bodies help porcupines to **feel** their way in the dark.

Bats

A special sense of **hearing** means that bats can find an insect to eat even though they can't see it.

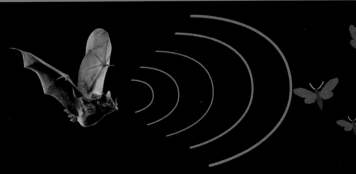

Twit-twoo! Some owls hoot and others screeech!

Big eyes help owls to **see** in the dark.

Did you know?

Animals that sleep during the day and come out at night are called nocturnal.

Owls

These night-time birds are amazing hunters. Owls fly silently, so their prey can't hear them coming.

Long sharp claws grab and hold onto small animals.

23

Pinecone owl

Make a **googly eyed** pinecone owl. You can tie a piece of **thread** around the top and hang it up.

You will need:

Coloured felt

Scissors

PVA glue

Googly eyes

Pinecone

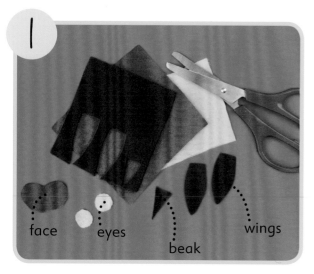

1

face   eyes   beak   wings

Ask an adult to help you cut a face, two eyes, a beak, and two wings from felt. Use the picture as a guide.

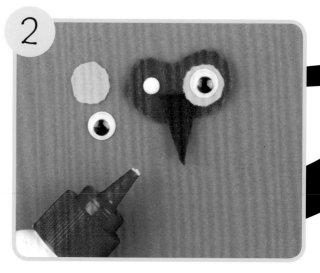

2

Stick the beak onto the face. Add a circle on either side and stick a googly eye on each of the felt eyes.

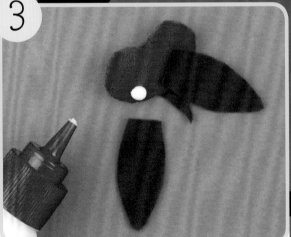

3

When the glue has dried, turn the felt over and glue down the two wings.

4

Leave everything until it is completely dry. Now stick the felt to the upside down cone to make your owl.

Leaf buds in spring

Seasons

There are four seasons in a year. As the weather changes in each season, a **deciduous** tree will first grow and then lose its leaves.

Spring

Spring is a time of new life. Animals are born, and trees start to grow new leaves and flowers.

Summer

In warm and sunny summer, trees are full of big green leaves. Insects flutter around flowers.

Maple leaf in autumn

Maple seeds

Maple leaf in summer

Maple seeds

These seeds have "wings" that catch the wind. They spin to the ground like helicopters, and grow into a new tree.

Autumn

The days become cooler in autumn. Leaves turn golden, red, and brown as they dry up and fall off the trees.

Winter

The weather turns chilly in winter. The trees have no leaves left. New leaves will grow again when the sun comes out in the spring.

27

Winter wonders

Forest animals have **clever tricks** for coping with the cold and lack of food in **winter.**

Moose

Growing a thicker coat in winter helps moose to stay warm.

Stoats

In very snowy winters, stoats turn white. When they are the same colour as the snow their enemies can't see them.

 Stoat's summer coat

Hoarders

Squirrels bury nuts and seeds in the autumn and dig them up in the winter when the trees are bare.

Many birds fly to somewhere warmer in the winter.

Brown bears find shelter in a cave or dig a den for themselves.

Acorns buried by squirrels

ZZZZZZZZZZZZ

zzzzzz

Forest mice curl up into a little ball and go to sleep to keep warm.

Big sleep

Lots of animals escape the cold by having a nice long sleep. Sometimes they sleep all winter without any food or water!

29

Bear mask

Grrrrr! Pretend to be a bear with this easy-to-make **furry** bear mask. Don't forget to **growl!**

You will need:

2 paper plates
Scissors
Brown tissue paper
Paintbrush
PVA glue
Black marker pen
Sticky tape
Short stick

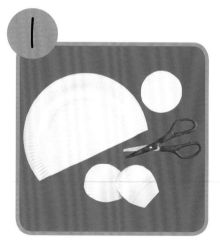

1

Cut a third off a paper plate. Then cut out a circle and two ear shapes from the other plate.

2

Tear the brown paper into little pieces and glue them onto the paper plate and ears.

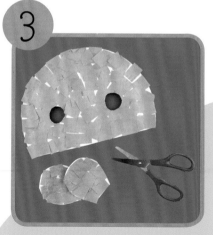

3

Ask an adult to cut two holes for eyes.

4

Draw a nose and mouth on the circle using the marker pen. Then colour in a black patch on each ear.

5

Glue the circle onto your mask leaving a little bit sticking out at the bottom.

6

Turn the mask over and tape the top of the stick to one side. Try on your mask!

Index

Acknowledgements

The publisher would like to thank the following for their kind permission to reproduce their photographs:

(Key: a-above; b-below/bottom; c-centre; f-far; l-left; r-right; t-top)

1 Dorling Kindersley: Jerry Young (cb). 2 Alamy Stock Photo: Peter Llewellyn (L) (crb). 4 Getty Images: VWB photos (cra). 8 Alamy Stock Photo: EyeEm Mobile GmbH (clb). naturepl.com: Georgette Douwma (crb). 9 naturepl.com: Adam Burton (crb). 10 Getty Images: Donald M. Jones / Minden Pictures (bc); Sean Russell (cla). 11 Alamy Stock Photo: All Canada Photos (cla); Hilda DeSanctis (b); Peter Llewellyn (L) (crb). Getty Images: Mai Tsugihara (ca). naturepl.com: Visuals Unlimited (cl). 19 Dorling Kindersley: Jerry Young (ca). 21 Getty Images: Mike Kemp (cla).

22 Alamy Stock Photo: Design Pics Inc (br). Dorling Kindersley: Jerry Young (cr). 23 naturepl.com: Loic Poidevin (fclb). 26 Getty Images: artland (crb); Picavet (cb). naturepl.com: Colin Varndell (tc). 26-27 Getty Images: George Diebold (t). 27 Alamy Stock Photo: Andrew Sabai (br); Errka / Stockimo (cr). naturepl.com: Martin Gabriel (bl); Nick Upton (cra). 28 naturepl.com: Andy Rouse (crb); Erlend Haarberg (bl). 29 naturepl.com: Andy Rouse (crb); George Sanker (ca)

Cover images: Front: Alamy Stock Photo: Peter Llewellyn (L) cb/ (Bird); **Fotolia:** Stefan Andronache (cb); **Getty Images:** Sean Russell (flb); Back: **Dorling Kindersley:** British Wildlife Centre, Surrey, UK cl, E. J. Peiker (cra)

All other images © Dorling Kindersley
For further information see: www.dkimages.com